NBA CHAMPIONS ATLANTA HAWKS

NBA CHAMPIONS

ATLANTA HAWKS

AARON FRISCH

CREATIVE EDUCATION

Published by Creative Education
P.O. Box 227, Mankato, Minnesota 56002
Creative Education is an imprint of The Creative Company
www.thecreativecompany.us

Book and cover design by Blue Design (www.bluedes.com)
Art direction by Rita Marshall
Printed by Corporate Graphics in the United States of
America

Photographs by AP Images, Getty Images (Andrew D.
Bernstein/NBAE, Nathaniel S. Butler/NBAE, Scott
Cunningham/NBAE, Jerry Driendl, Jesse D. Garrabrant/
NBAE, Noah Graham/NBAE, Walter Iooss Jr./NBAE, George
Long/WireImage, Fernando Medina/NBAE, Richard Meek/
Sports Illustrated, Bob Rosato/Sports Illustrated)

Library of Congress Cataloging-in-Publication Data

Frisch, Aaron.
Atlanta Hawks / by Aaron Frisch.
p. cm. — (NBA champions)
Includes bibliographical references and index.
Summary: A basic introduction to the Atlanta Hawks
professional basketball team, including its formation
as the Tri-Cities Blackhawks in 1946, greatest players,
championship, and stars of today.
ISBN 978-1-60818-130-8
1. Atlanta Hawks (Basketball team)—History—Juvenile
literature. I. Title.
GV885.52.A7F75 2011
796.323'6409758231—dc22   2010050544

CPSIA: 030111 PO1448

First edition
9 8 7 6 5 4 3 2 1

3 1907 00312 9730

Cover: Josh Smith
Page 2: Al Horford
Right: Bob Pettit
Page 6: Mike Bibby

TABLE OF CONTENTS

Ted Turner was the owner of the Hawks for 24 years

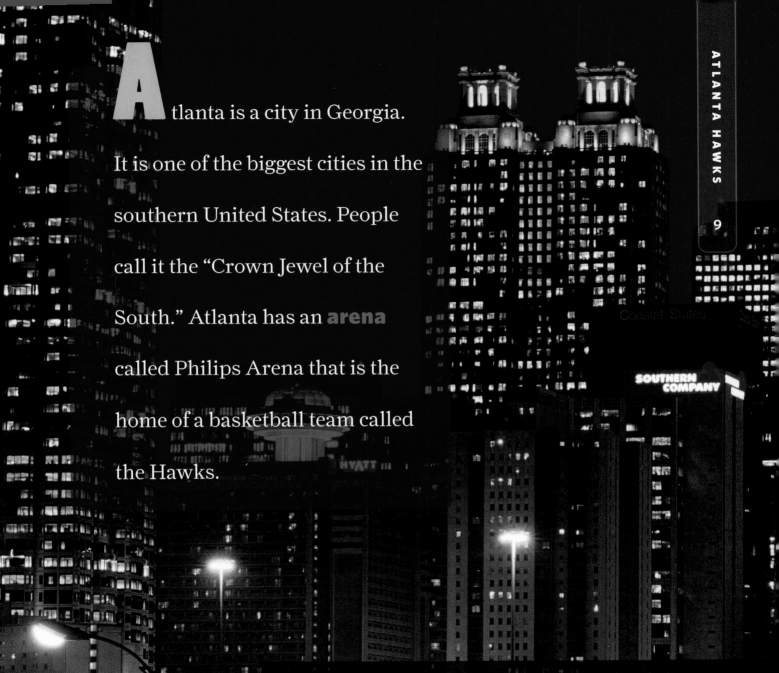

Atlanta is a city in Georgia. It is one of the biggest cities in the southern United States. People call it the "Crown Jewel of the South." Atlanta has an **arena** called Philips Arena that is the home of a basketball team called the Hawks.

Philips Arena is close to many tall skyscrapers in Atlanta

The Hawks are part of the National Basketball Association (NBA). All the teams in the NBA try to win the **NBA Finals** to become world champions. The Hawks play many games against teams called the Bobcats, Heat, Magic, and Wizards.

The Hawks started playing in 1946. They played home games in Illinois and Iowa then and were called the Tri-Cities Blackhawks. They moved to Milwaukee, Wisconsin, in 1951. Milwaukee fans cheered for players like center Chuck Share.

Cliff Hagan made many baskets after grabbing rebounds

The Hawks moved to St. Louis, Missouri, in 1955. Forward Cliff Hagan scored a lot of points to help make St. Louis a great team. The Hawks got to the NBA Finals in 1957 and 1958. They lost the first time but won the championship in 1958!

SAY IT LIKE THIS

Hagan
HAY-gen

Tree Rollins was 7-foot-1 and weighed almost 300 pounds

In 1968, the Hawks moved to Atlanta. Center Tree Rollins blocked a lot of shots, and the Hawks got to the **playoffs** many times. But they could not win the championship again.

HAWKS FACTS

- Started playing: 1946
- Conference/division: Eastern Conference, Southeast Division
- Team colors: navy, red, and silver
- NBA championship:

  1958 — 4 games to 2 versus Boston Celtics
- NBA Web site for kids: http://www.nba.com/kids/

Why Are They Called the Hawks?
A fight between American Indians and the United States Army happened in Illinois and Iowa in 1832. The fight was called the Black Hawk War. When the Blackhawks moved to Milwaukee in 1951, they shortened their name to just "Hawks."

Quick guard Spud Webb helped make the Hawks an exciting team in the 1980s and 1990s. In 2004–05, Atlanta won just 13 games and lost 69. But the Hawks got better after that.

Spud Webb was one of the shortest NBA players (5-foot-7)

Hawks stars Bob Pettit (above) and Lou Hudson (opposite)

Two of the Hawks' first stars were forward/center Bob Pettit and **swingman** Lou Hudson. Pettit was a tough rebounder in the 1950s and 1960s. Hudson scored many points using his excellent jump shot.

SAY IT LIKE THIS

Pettit
PET-it

Dominique Wilkins played for Atlanta for 12 seasons

Forward Dominique Wilkins joined Atlanta in 1982. Fans loved to watch him score with amazing slam dunks. Forward Josh Smith became another high-jumping Hawks star.

SAY IT LIKE THIS

Dominique
dah-mih-NEEK

Josh Smith was only 18 years old when he joined the NBA

Joe Johnson and the Hawks won 4 playoff games in 2010

In 2005, Atlanta added Joe Johnson. He was a big guard who played in the **All-Star Game** every year from 2007 to 2011. Atlanta fans hoped that he would help lead the Hawks to their second NBA championship!

GLOSSARY

All-Star Game — a special game in the middle of the season that only the best players get to play

arena — a large building for indoor sports events; it has many seats for fans

navy — a color that is very dark blue

NBA Finals — a series of games between two teams at the end of the playoffs; the first team to win four games is the champion

playoffs — games that the best teams play after a season

swingman — a basketball player who can play as a guard or forward

INDEX